GAINING MOMENTUM IN A DOWNTURN

A Recession Survival Guide For Retirees

CHRISTOPHER HOLMES

Copyright © 2022 CHRISTOPHER HOLMES

All rights reserved

The characters and events portrayed in this book are fictitious. Any similarity to real persons, living or dead, is coincidental and not intended by the author.

No part of this book may be reproduced, or stored in a retrieval system, or transmitted in any form or by any means, electronic, mechanical, photocopying, recording, or otherwise, without express written permission of the publisher.

CONTENTS

Title Page
Copyright
CHAPTER 1 — 1
CHAPTER 2 — 6
CHAPTER 3 — 12
CHAPTER 4 — 20
CHAPTER 5 — 27

CHAPTER 1

A recession is a period of time when the economy shrinks, as measured by gross domestic product. A recession typically lasts for at least six months and is often accompanied by high unemployment and falling stock prices.

Recessions can occur when a sudden significant decline (economic shock) in demand for goods and services or a financial crisis. While recessions are often difficult for businesses and individuals, they can lead to new opportunities as businesses adapt and innovate to survive.

Ultimately, recessions are a natural part of the economic cycle and provide an opportunity for economies to reset and grow long-term.

How Does A Recession Work?
A recession occurs when there is a decrease in the Gross Domestic Product (GDP) for two consecutive quarters. This means that the economy is not growing as it should. During this time, businesses tend to slow down economic activity or stop production, which leads to layoffs. As more people lose their jobs, unemployment rates go up.
Such a slowdown in economic activities may last

for some quarters thereby completely hampering the growth of an economy. In such a situation, economic indicators such as GDP, corporate profits, employment, etc., fall.

This creates a mess in the entire economy. To tackle the menace, economies generally react by loosening their monetary policies by infusing more money into the system, i.e., by increasing the money supply.

This is done by reducing the interest rates. Increased spending by the government and decreased taxation are also considered good answers to this problem. The recession which hit the globe in 2008 is the most recent example of a recession.

What Causes A Recession?
Many factors can cause a recession. Some of the most common causes include:

- A significant decline in economic activity (consumer spending)
- An increase in interest rates from the Federal Reserve Bank
- A decrease in business investment
- A stock market crash

There is more than one way for a recession to get started, from a sudden economic shock to fallout from uncontrolled inflation. These phenomena are some of the main drivers of a recession:

A sudden economic shock: An economic shock is a

surprise problem that creates serious financial damage. In the 1970s, OPEC cut off the supply of oil to the U.S. without warning, causing a recession, not to mention endless lines at gas stations. The coronavirus outbreak, which shut down economies worldwide, is a more recent example of a sudden economic shock.

Excessive debt: When individuals or businesses take on too much debt, the cost of servicing the debt can grow to the point where they can't pay their bills. Growing debt defaults and bankruptcies then capsize the economy. The housing bubble in the mid-aughts that led to the Great Recession is a prime example of excessive debt causing a recession.

Asset bubbles: When investing decisions are driven by emotion, bad economic outcomes aren't far behind. Investors can become too optimistic during a strong economy. Irrational exuberance inflates stock market or real estate bubbles—and when the bubbles pop, panic selling can crash the market, causing a recession.

Too much inflation: Inflation is the steady, upward trend in prices over time. Inflation isn't a bad thing per se, but excessive inflation is a dangerous phenomenon. Central banks control inflation by raising interest rates, and higher interest rates depress economic activity. Out-of-control inflation was an ongoing problem in the U.S. in the 1970s. To break the cycle, the Federal Reserve rapidly raised interest rates, which caused a recession.

Too much deflation: While runaway inflation can create a recession, deflation can be even worse. Deflation is when prices decline over time, which causes wages to contract, which further depresses prices. When a deflationary feedback loop gets out of hand, people and businesses stop spending, which undermines the economy. Central banks and economists have few tools to fix the underlying problems that cause deflation. Japan's struggles with deflation throughout most of the 1990s caused a severe recession.

Technological change: New inventions increase productivity and help the economy over the long term, but there can be short-term periods of adjustment to technological breakthroughs. In the 19th century, there were waves of labor-saving technological improvements. The Industrial Revolution made entire professions obsolete, sparking recessions and hard times. Today, some economists worry that AI and robots could cause recessions by eliminating whole categories of jobs.

What Is the Duration of a Recession?

When a country's gross domestic product (GDP) has two consecutive quarters of negative economic growth, this is referred to as a recession (GDP).

What is the duration of a recession? The longest recession in American history lasted 18 months, from December 2007 to June 2009. However, depending on the nation and the economic slump, recessions may range in duration. For instance, the post-financial crisis recession in Iceland barely lasted six months, but the recession in Greece lasted more than six years.

In the end, a number of variables, including the nations involved, the severity of the economic slump, and governmental measures, affect how long a recession lasts.

One thing is for certain, though: going through a recession is never fun. High unemployment rates, declining wages, and increasing prices are often present in tandem with them. As a consequence, it is always preferable to stay away from them.

Market Bear vs. Recession
Few things are more alarming for investors than a bear market. Since the earth may seem to abruptly change under your feet, it may be difficult to know what to do next. Bear in mind, however, that a recession and a bear market are not the same things.

Two consecutive quarters of negative economic growth are considered to constitute a recession, which often results in a bear market. A bear market, however, may also happen in the absence of a recession.

A bear market may be started, for instance, by a sharp decline in consumer confidence or a rise in interest rates. Therefore, even while a recession is a cause for worry, it's crucial to keep in mind that a bear market is not always the same.

CHAPTER 2

What Can You Do To Get Ready For A Recession?

There are certain things you can do to be ready if a recession is something you're worried about. Here are some pointers:

Try to accumulate an emergency fund that can cover three to six months of living costs to help you be ready for a recession, job loss, or another financial challenge.
Reach out to your creditors if you're having trouble making your debt payments and request hardship concessions.

Identify your top financial priorities.
Uncertainty about what will happen next and when things will improve is one of the worst aspects of a recession. Therefore, it's critical to understand your financial situation. As you evaluate your financial status, ask yourself these important questions.

How much money do I currently have?
How much money can I fast access if I need it?
How much debt (school loans, credit cards, etc.) do I presently have?
What are my basic monthly living costs, including

daycare, transportation, housing, and health insurance? Do you have any important life events (such as marriages, having a kid, or retiring) coming up that may incur substantial costs?

Understanding your current expenditures and planning for your requirements for the next six months should be done right now. You'll have an emergency fund that can cover three to six months of living expenditures if you are adequately prepared for a recession, a job loss, or other financial challenges (and hopefully a healthy nest egg for retirement).

Set it as your financial objective if you don't have enough cash on hand to cover your basic costs for at least three to six months. Create a budget and start by getting a basic grasp of how you are spending your money.

Calculate the entire household income from all sources, including your own, that of your partner(s), and any additional money from side jobs. Include investment income as well as any other sources of income, such as child support.

Then, make a list of all of your regular monthly expenses, including your rent or mortgage, utilities, groceries, prescription, and medical costs, childcare expenses, home, and auto maintenance, debt payments, insurance premiums, and any other recurring costs, even those that you only incur once a year. To determine if you're spending more, less, or about the same as your monthly take-home income, add up everything.

In case you or your spouse/partner has a job loss, be

sure to prioritize your critical costs and determine the absolute lowest you can spend each month to get by.

It's acceptable if your budget has to change in advance of a recession. Spend less on entertainment, cable, and apparel if at all possible. Even if it's impractical to expect you can eliminate all discretionary expenditure, it's crucial to distinguish between necessities and desires. Find any places where you could have gone over budget. Try to determine what caused it. It's okay in the near run if you don't have any extra cash on hand right now to contribute to your retirement or a down payment.

You're off to a fantastic start if you make it a habit to analyze your money and seek issue areas.

If you can, prioritize paying off your debts.
You could be concerned about clearing up unpaid obligations like credit card balances, utility payments, or school loans in the next months. It's important to know which bills you must pay since you may have to skip paying one or more of them if your income is lost.

For instance, if you lose your job, you may not be able to pay all of your bills each month on time or in full. Your credit ratings will be directly impacted by this.

In a normal economy, it's essential to take all reasonable steps to maintain your credit ratings, but this may not be attainable during a recession. So that you may pay off as many debts as possible with the money you have available, you should prioritize how you pay your expenses.

Make careful to make prompt and complete rent or mortgage payments. Avoid foreclosure or eviction at all costs.

Pay your automobile loan, particularly if you depend on a vehicle to travel to work.

If your income is going to decrease, get in touch with your student loan provider and request a hardship application. This might give you a few months without having to make a payment.

Make your credit card's minimum payment at the very least. If that isn't feasible, get in touch with your credit card provider and attempt to arrange a payment schedule. (Just be aware that the creditor will probably freeze your accounts, preventing you from using the card to make any more transactions.)

If you can, continue making payments on your medical bills, but only after other obligations have been satisfied. If your work provides health insurance, you will continue to have access to it even if your medical expenses increase. Regardless of whether you're self-employed or purchasing health insurance for any other reason, be sure to pay your premiums on time to avoid having your coverage canceled.

Remember to contact your creditors and request hardship concessions if you find yourself in financial trouble. This can include deferral of payments or making interest-only payments on your loan.

For a personal loan, you may also inquire at your neighborhood bank or credit union. In times of need, your company could also provide a short-term loan program in addition to internet lenders.

You may also request a reduction in interest rates from your credit card company or any other lender if you're making on-time payments. Many large utility companies provide programs that can let you postpone payment of your bills or give other hardship relief. If you don't inquire, you'll never know what kind of arrangement you and your creditor can achieve.

Think about your present and future professional options.
High unemployment rates are a common side effect of recessions. As a result, it's crucial to think about how difficult economic circumstances can affect your job and have a backup plan in place in case you are laid off.

Refresh your professional network's relationships first. Think about your relationships both within and outside of your present workplace, as well as with your colleagues. Having connections at several firms might provide you with a significant advantage in the employment market. You may think about contacting your network on social media or proposing to meet up for coffee in person.

Update your CV and other job-hunting materials in advance if possible. Look for any gaps as you review your prior work experience. Are there any locations where you might seek extra training or ongoing education? One of the finest ways to invest in yourself as a worker is to increase your skill set. Even if you manage to hold onto your job during a recession, this is still true.

It could be advantageous for certain employees who are concerned about being laid off to start a side business like freelancing or working for a ridesharing service. In addition to helping in the case of a layoff, having a second source of income might make it simpler to save emergency funds while you are still working.

Try to increase your emergency savings in advance.
Even if job losses or layoffs are imminent, put as much money as you can into your emergency fund. When the revenue stops coming in, you'll need every last piece of it. Give up anything extra, including delivery and takeout.

Losing your work or having to live on lower wage counts as a solid reason to utilize part of the money you've saved, but it's never a choice you should make lightly. However, as soon as your financial condition improves, it's critical to replenish your emergency money. If not, you could be forced to make difficult choices like taking money out of your retirement account or asking for a home equity line of credit when the next emergency arises.

Maintaining awareness of your financial status is important.
Even though a recession may be a challenging period, the greatest thing you can do is start proactively preparing for it now. Financial literacy is crucial now more than ever so you can feel confident about your financial situation no matter what obstacles lie ahead.

CHAPTER 3

What To Do In A Recession

Many people are feeling anxious about the current state of the economy. While it's normal to feel some uncertainty during times of economic upheaval, there are some things you can do to help weather the storm.

One of the most important things you can do is to stay informed. Keep up with the latest news and developments to make informed decisions about your finances. Additionally, it's important to create a budget and stick to it. Make sure you're only spending money on essential items, and try to save as much as possible.

Recessions can be difficult, but by taking some proactive steps, you can help reduce the impact on your life. Stay informed, budget carefully, and be mindful of your spending, and you'll be on your way to weathering the storm.

What To Invest In During A Recession

Wondering how to invest with a recession coming? Many think investing in fixed-rate investments like bonds during a recession is best. However, fixed indexed annuities can be a better choice. With a fixed indexed annuity, you earn interest based on the performance of a stock index, but your investment is fixed, so you don't have to worry about losing money if the stock market crashes.

This makes them a great option for people who are worried about the potential for another recession. In addition, fixed indexed annuities often have higher interest rates than bonds, so you can potentially earn more money on your investment.

How To Recession-Proof Your Retirement
Suppose you are retired or close to it; you may wonder how to prepare for a recession. After all, an economic downturn can significantly impact your retirement income and lifestyle. Here are a few tips to help you weather the storm:

Review your budget and expenses: One of the first things you should do is look closely at your budget and expenses. Determine what items are essential and what can be cut back on or eliminated. This will help you free up some cash flow to help cover unexpected expenses during recessions.

Build an emergency fund: An emergency fund can be a lifesaver. This fund can help you cover unexpected expenses, such as a job loss or medical bills. Build up your emergency fund to cover at least three to six months of living expenses.

Invest in recession-proof Investments: Another way to prepare is to invest in less likely assets impacted by an economic downturn. For example, you may want to consider investing in fixed and fixed index annuities, bonds, or other less volatile investments.

Stay diversified: It's also important to stay diversified with your investments. This means not putting all of your eggs in one basket. By diversifying, you can help reduce your overall risk and potentially increase your chances of weathering a global recession.

Have a plan: Finally, it's essential to have a plan in place if you experience financial difficulties during an economic recession. This plan should include how you will pay your bills, cut back on expenses, and what you will do if you lose your job. A plan can help reduce stress and give you a sense of control during an uncertain time. While an economic decline can be brutal for everyone, retirees may face unique challenges. However, by following these tips, you can help ensure that you are prepared for the future.

What Are The Effects Of A Recession?

An economic shock can affect individuals, businesses, and the economy as a whole. Some of the most common effects include:

Increased unemployment rate: As businesses lay off workers, unemployment rates increase.

Decreased consumer spending: When people are unemployed or worried about losing their jobs, they tend to spend less money.

Decreased business investment: Businesses may slow down or stop production altogether, leading to even more layoffs.

What Are The Warning Signs Of A Recession?

A few economic indicators signaling a recession may be on the horizon. These include:

An increase in jobless claims: This is one of the first signs that unemployment is rising.
A decrease in retail sales: As consumers cut back on spending, businesses may see a decrease in sales.
An increase in foreclosures: If more people are unable to make their mortgage payments, this is a sign that the economy is struggling.
A decrease in stock prices: When asset prices fall in the financial markets can be a sign that investors are losing consumer confidence in the economy.

However, if you are concerned about the possibility of an economic downturn, you can take steps to protect your retirement plan.

Here are a few tips:

Save regularly and make sure you have an emergency fund. This will help you weather any short-term economic downturns.

Stay diversified: This means having a mix of different types of investments in your portfolio. This way, if one investment goes down, you will still have others doing well.

Consider investing in conservative investments such as bonds and cash equivalents. These will not lose value if the stock market crashes.

Finally, consider a deferred annuity with a lifetime income rider. An annuity is a retirement plan that will provide you with a stream of income you cannot outlive, no matter how long you live and the state of the economy.

What Happens If We Go Into A Recession?

If the economy weakens sharply and unemployment rises significantly, we will likely enter a recession. This extended period will last a minimum of two consecutive quarters of negative economic growth measured by a country's gross domestic product. A recessionary period is typically accompanied by a drop in the financial markets, an increase in foreclosures and personal bankruptcies, and a decrease in consumer spending and business investment.

While an economic decline may not sound good news, it's important to remember that economies constantly fluctuate. As such, recessions are a normal part of the business cycle. Moreover, they can be helpful in the long run by helping to cleanse the economy of excesses and imbalances.

Nonetheless, recessions can also cause short-term hardship for businesses and consumers alike. Therefore, it's essential to be prepared financially if we enter a recessionary period.

How Can I Protect My 401(K) From A Recession?

There are a few things you can do to protect your 401(k) from a recession:

First, review your asset allocation and make sure it is diversified.

When it comes to investing, one of the most critical

considerations is asset allocation. This refers to the mix of different types of investments in your portfolio, which can significantly impact your overall financial health. For example, if you invest all of your money in stocks, you may see strong growth in the short term, but you will also be at greater risk of losses in a downturn.

On the other hand, investing too heavily in bonds can provide stability but limit your upside potential. The key is to strike a balance that meets your needs and helps you reach your financial goals. In addition, reviewing your asset allocation regularly can help ensure that you are still diversified and positioned for success.

Consider investing in stable value funds.
When it comes to investing, there are many different options to choose from. However, one type of investment that is often overlooked is stable value funds. While they may not offer the potential for high returns, they can provide a measure of stability in an otherwise volatile market. For example, if you are retired and living on a fixed income, stable value funds can help ensure that your nest egg lasts as long as you need it.

In addition, if you are concerned about market turbulence, stable value funds can provide a way to protect your capital. Of course, as with any investment, there is no guarantee that you will make money from investing in stable value funds. However, they may be worth considering if you are looking for a way to preserve your capital and generate a steady income.

Stay disciplined with your contributions.

Getting caught up in the daily grind and forgetting about our long-term goals can be easy. For example, we may tell ourselves that we'll start saving for retirement next month or eventually pay off our credit card debt obligations. However, these delays can end up costing us dearly in the future. That's why it's so important to stay disciplined with our contributions.

By setting aside a fixed amount each month and investing it wisely, we can ensure that we're on track to reach our financial goals. And while it may require some short-term sacrifices, the peace of mind that comes from knowing we're prepared for the future is worth it. So give yourself a boost today by staying disciplined with your contributions. It's one of the best things you can do for your financial well-being.

Avoid making any rash decisions.
One of the most important things to remember in life is to avoid making any rash decisions due to an economic shock. A rash decision is defined as a decision made without careful thought or consideration. This can often lead to regret, whether immediately afterward or further down the road. Rash decisions are often made in the heat of the moment when we feel emotional or under pressure.

In these situations, taking a step back and taking time to think things through before making a final decision is essential. So often, rash decisions are made on impulse, and we later realize that they were not the best choice. If we can learn to slow down and think through our choices, we can avoid rash decisions that we may regret later.

Consider a fixed indexed annuity.

A fixed indexed annuity is an insurance contract that provides a guaranteed minimum interest rate and the potential to earn additional interest based on the performance of one or more underlying indexes like the S&P 500 Dow Jones, and Nasdaq while offering protection from market downturns while providing the opportunity for growth during periods of market expansion

The first to go are pre-retirees

Even while losing a job during a recession is terrible for everyone, pre-retirees often lose their jobs first. Companies are searching for methods to reduce expenses and save money. They may do this by getting rid of untenable jobs, many of which are filled by senior employees. For pre-retirees who rely on their work to provide retirement income, this may be a major setback.

CHAPTER 4

Recession-Proof Investments For Retirement

You may take a few steps to make your retirement plan recession-proof.

First, make sure your investment portfolio is diverse. In this manner, even if one investment fails, you will still have others that are profitable.

Continue to diversify, second. This entails incorporating a variety of investment kinds into your portfolio. In this manner, even if one investment fails, you will still have others that are profitable.

Third, think about making investments in safe securities like bonds and cash equivalents. In the event of a stock market meltdown, they won't lose value.

Consider a delayed annuity with a lifetime income rider as the last option. No matter how long you live or the status of the economy, an annuity is a retirement strategy that will provide you with a steady source of income.

Smart Ways to Secure Guaranteed Retirement Income

At first look, it could seem to be a daunting task, but you have several alternatives for securing your retirement income. Some may be last-minute decisions made just before you decide to stop working, while others are better suited to long-term preparation. Your finest outcomes could be obtained by combining the two.

Depending on whether you're young and just starting to save or you're searching for a plan later in life, your choices for protecting your income in retirement may differ.
You may receive money from annuities now or in the future. You have the power to decide.
If your first mortgage has been paid off or you have a sizable amount of equity in it, getting a reverse mortgage can be beneficial.
Planning for retirement income includes avoiding certain frequent Social Security errors, which is a key element.

Purchase a Direct Annuity
The simplest approach to getting a guaranteed retirement income is to... Buy it. This is precisely what you do when you acquire an instant annuity. Your purchase of guaranteed income is made with a flat amount of cash.

If you're married, you may pick an option where the income is paid out throughout both of your lives. For those hoping to live to 100, the purchase might be the opportunity of a lifetime! With an instant annuity, you cannot outlive your income.

The greatest time to consider this choice is when you're ready to retire since, as the name indicates, "instant" means the income begins immediately away. You need a source of revenue that can start right now. Your age will determine just how much money you may get each month. The amount of income you get for every dollar invested increases with age.

Utilize a Deferred Annuity's Withdrawal Benefit Rider.
If you want to buy assured retirement income in the future, look for an annuity that includes a guaranteed minimum withdrawal benefit rider (also known as a GMWB) or a lifetime withdrawal benefit (an LWB).

With the purpose of withdrawing income in ten years or more, you deposit your money now. Every year as you go along, the annuity provider takes a snapshot of the value of your account. As the account value increases, the new, higher value is fixed as the new "income basis." When you activate your withdrawal rider, your guaranteed withdrawals will be generated using whichever figure is greater—the current account value or the income base value.

Usually, you may withdraw between 4% and 6% of the account value or income base value. Your age at the time of withdrawal and the conditions of your contract will determine the precise percentage.

If you have 10 to 15 years before retirement, using this option may be an excellent method to shield account assets from the effects of a significant market collapse. This is especially true if the deterioration occurs as you approach retirement age.

Attempt to Obtain a Pension

A pension upon retirement is wonderful. Some professionals work in a government organization for the last ten years of their employment only to get one. For individuals who didn't save enough for retirement early in their careers, it's a wise choice. Find companies that provide pensions, then research the vesting timeline for those companies.

If you're considering changing jobs and waiting a little longer will provide you with more assured retirement income, you may choose to do so. Your retirement may be more secure with the aid of these decisions.

Some individuals fear that they may not get all the perks they were promised from their pensions. Your retirement income will be more secure the older you are when you begin receiving it. The Pension Benefit Guarantee Corporation, or PBGC, is a kind of government insurance.

It safeguards pension payments, but there is a limit to the amount that is guaranteed.

For each year you retire before age 65, the covered amount is decreased. To maximize the insured amount if your pension is protected by the PBGC, start receiving benefits at age 65 or later.

Apply for a reverse mortgage
Retirement income that is guaranteed is just that: risk-free income you can rely on for the rest of your life. That amount of protection may be offered by a reverse mortgage, and the income is tax-free. So why aren't they used by more people? Fear and costs are two causes.

People first worry that the bank may seize their house. This was true in the past, but since around 1985, restrictions have altered significantly. This product is now more durable, risk-free, and safe for the borrower.

Second, some individuals believe the costs to be too costly. Regulations have once again made this situation better. No longer are fees permitted to exceed governmental limits. If you are 62 years of age or older, in need of a guaranteed retirement income, and own your house outright or with significant equity, a reverse mortgage may be a possibility.

Be cautious while submitting a Social Security claim.
Social Security accounts for the majority of pensioners' guaranteed earnings. A cost-of-living adjustment is given to those receiving Social Security benefits every year, and it often increases payments.

The issue is that the majority of individuals still claim their Social Security benefits too early or, if they are married, do so without consulting their spouse. Because one spouse made a poor choice on when to start receiving benefits, hundreds of thousands of dollars in income that would have been given out in the form of spousal benefits and widow/widower benefits may have been lost.

Avoid applying for Social Security benefits at age 62. Beginning benefits later in life can often result in a better outcome for you and greater lifetime guaranteed income.

Longevity insurance is a kind of deferred immediate annuity that will provide you a certain level of income at a certain future age, such as 85 or 90.

This product is available in a unique variant known as a QLAC or Qualified Longevity Annuity Contract. It is bought using an IRA or 401(k) (k). You can postpone the beginning of your mandatory minimum distributions using the QLAC.

Because they know they will have a future source of guaranteed income to support them later, people with longevity insurance feel safer about using their retirement funds now for pleasure and travel.

Construct a Bond Ladder
Many retirees are reluctant to spend their principal, but if done correctly as part of a plan, it can be just fine.

You may create a ladder out of bonds or CDs. This entails investing in a certificate of deposit or bond that will mature in the year in which you will need the money to pay for expenses. You have to spend the bond when it matures.

Utilizing Treasury securities is an alternative option. These government-issued bonds from the United States are among the safest investments you can make. Financial institutions can separate the bond's principal and interest components, a process known as Treasury STRIPS. These strips may be purchased with maturities that are laddered out, generating a stream of income that is assured to mature in the year that you need it.

Future Steps

Everyone might suffer greatly during a recession, but it's important to keep in mind that your retirement plan can still be protected. Make sure you have an emergency fund, stay diversified, and think about investing in conservative securities if you are worried about the state of the economy.

By implementing these suggestions, you can increase the likelihood that your retirement plan will withstand the test and give you the security you require financially during this trying time.

CHAPTER 5

Frequently asked questions

When will there be a recession?
It is difficult to know for certain. However, a lot of analysts predict that a recession will occur in 2023.

What consequences does the recession have?
The results might be disastrous. For instance, a downturn in the economy may result in firm closures, higher unemployment rates, and lower consumer spending.

What affects the stock market during a recession?
The stock market might collapse during recessions.

What should I do if a recession strikes?
You should safeguard your retirement plan if a recession is something you're worried about. This might include making regular savings, maintaining a diverse portfolio, and making prudent investment choices. As the economy starts to improve, you may also want to think about investing in a fixed index annuity to secure your assets and receive a return.

What does the term "recession" mean?
Typically, two consecutive quarters of negative economic growth constitute a recession.

Why does inflation occur before a recession?
Because the Federal Reserve Bank boosts interest rates to slow the economy and avoid inflation, a recession often follows inflation. An economic downturn may result from a substantial decline in economic activity as a result of this.

Where should I put my money in a recession?
During a slump in the economy, you can think about buying bonds and cash equivalents. In the event of a stock market meltdown, they won't lose value. A fixed or fixed index annuity may also be something you want to think about as they provide both market volatility protection and the chance to earn money.

Which assets are immune to recessions?
Because they are unaffected by the stock market, fixed index annuities are the most recession-proof investment because bonds and gold may change in value as a result of market circumstances. Similar to Social Security Benefits, FIAs may provide you with a reliable source of income that won't end when you do.

Is cash useful during a recession?
Yes, it's wise to always have cash on hand. For instance, you could need enough money to pay your bills for three to six months. This will enable you to handle any financial difficulties that may arise.

What distinguishes depression from a recession?
Recessions are not as bad as depressions. A prolonged period of negative economic growth known as depression is frequently accompanied by rising

unemployment and a decline in consumer spending. Recessions, on the other hand, are often milder and shorter.

What advantages do recessions have?
Economic recessions may not sound nice, but they are a typical feature of the business cycle. Furthermore, these bad times may be beneficial in the long term since they assist to purge the economy of excesses and imbalances.

What negative effects might a recession have?
Increased unemployment, lower consumer spending, and firm closures are all negative effects of a recession. Any economic shock, however, has the potential to lead the financial markets to collapse.

Who gains from a recession?
A recession could be advantageous to certain individuals. For instance, you may be able to discover fantastic discounts during a recession if you're trying to purchase a property. Investors who make low-priced purchases and profit when the economy improves are still another example.

During a recession, should I cease making contributions to my 401(k)?
During a recession, a lot of individuals question what to do with their 401(k). Saving money can seem like a good plan, but there are some possible drawbacks.

For instance, you could pass up the chance to invest in potentially risky but ultimately lucrative assets as well as employer matching contributions.

Fixed indexed annuities, on the other hand, may provide a method to safeguard your funds while continuing to enjoy the advantages of market participation. Your capital is guaranteed with these annuities, and you may make market-linked interest payments depending on the performance of an underlying index. Fixed indexed annuities can therefore provide you with the best of both worlds: security from market losses and the chance to take part in market gains.

What should my retirement monthly income be?
Those 65 and over in the U.S. had an average retirement income of $47,357 in 2021; the word "median" denotes that half of all retirees had an income higher than this and the other half lower. Therefore, if your income was higher than the median, it may be regarded as "excellent" or at the very least better than it was for half of all retirees in this age range.

An annuity can you live off of it?
Depending on the annuity type(s) you choose and the timing of when you opt to get the largest payments, you may be able to live off an annuity. Additionally, your retirement costs play a significant role. Make a projected budget, then include any additional retirement income you foresee. Check to see if the annuity you've selected or are thinking about will be adequate to cover any shortfall.

www.ingramcontent.com/pod-product-compliance
Lightning Source LLC
Chambersburg PA
CBHW050324220526
45465CB00005B/2120